HEAVENS ABOVE

ABOUT THESE STORIES

These accounts or stories have an interesting background. Let me try to explain. Some time ago, back when I lived in Sydney, we had a clothing shop. As I recall, It was on a quiet day, that I suddenly had the desire to write down some accounts about souls and angels. I didn't question it at the time, although it felt a bit strange. I didn't actually have a writing pad, so I wrote them on some brown paper bags. I think there were about 10-12 stories altogether. Stories that involved many souls, a heavenly chamber and some angels. I'd never done that before and wondered where it all came from. At the time I felt compelled, somehow, to do it. It was quite an uplifting, yet strange feeling.

I kept these paper bags, then transferred these stories into my old computer. Might've even been an atari, remember them? I got on with my life, but added to these stories over the years.

I should make it clear, I don't actually claim to have any more knowledge about the subject than anyone else. It all just stemmed from the first promptings

I didn't actually know what to do with these accounts, but as said, kept them and edited and re edited them. I told my late mother about my angel stories. She was an immigrant to Australia, from Czechoslovakia, just prior to WW2. She came from the German speaking part, called Sudetenland. She told me how she recalled her paternal grandmother, a lady named Paula Lederer, was always writing stories about souls and angels. Apparently, similar to mine. "Wait," mum said, "I have some stories somewhere, I'm sure, from grandma Paula, let me look.." It wasn't long after that, that she sent me some thin old crumpled pieces of paper, with German old font type on them. Paula's stories. She had perished during the war, but was always attempting to write, despite the fact that she had about seven children.

I didn't understand the German, so took it to a friend who worked at SBS - the multicultural TV station in Sydney at the time. I said to the person I knew there, "would you mind having these translated for me please?" "Sure," she answered.

It wasn't long before they came back in English. As I read them, I was struck, by the similarities to my stories. There were angels and newly departed souls talking to them. One in particular, raised the hair on the back of my neck - it was called BEESWAX. It was almost identical to my story. How could this be? I still have no explanation. Perhaps she was acting from the other side and wanted me to continue her work. Who knows?

Since that time I've fiddled around with the stories, as said. Also put it off, until now. I am very conscious of the years passing by now and want to get it out there somehow. Hopefully people will enjoy the stories and get something positive out of them.

Many, I have rewritten in the last few weeks. Some, from the beginning, were just right, so I left them as they were. Essentially the same as when I wrote them on some paper bags. Others, needed more work.

thanks,
Pietr

ABOUT PIETR, THE AUTHOR

Well thats me. I was born in Perth West Australia but moved to the UK sometime ago, where I live with my wife. Primarily, I consider myself as a guitarist/songwriter. That's what I've been doing most of my life. Even though it's a while ago, Ive had my songs recorded by other artists. LOTTA ENGBERG, from sweden, THE BLIND BOYS OF ALABAMA (from guess where?) HOWLING BELLS the UK - lots of others. I love playing blues guitar as well.

The spiritual writing I enjoy as well, especially when a talented artist like Marie interprets the text. My books in that sense, so far anyhow, are adult picture books. Perhaps that will change in the future
My email is
shakeatambourine@gmail.com

The artwork - Marie Muravski

Marie is a very gifted artist from Poland. I gave her the text for the various stories and I feel she connected to the essence of these, interpreting them perfectly, in my opinion.
i hope you agree.
Also, she is involved with animal rights organisations.

A book by Pietr

Making a positive difference
shakeatambourine@gmail.com

HEAVENS ABOVE

LEAD

As he approached the heavenly chamber, a large angel stood before him. It happened to be a male angel. The soul bowed his head and asked, "may I enter?". The angel replied, "Did you walk the path of love?" Looking confused, the soul answered,
"Of course, all men knew me, I was a great figure at the Temple and prayed with great fervour for all to see. I was on the council of the wise and upheld the law."
The angel pointed out respectfully, that, that is not what he asked.
Then he turned his attention to a large text called THE GREAT TEXT OF SOULS, that was sitting on a wooden lectern nearby. It was extremely thick and also appeared to be very ancient. It had a wooden cover, an iron lock and a key that was attached by a piece of thin leather.

The angel studied the text for a time and then turned to the soul,

"Each act of love or kindness, is like a gold coin. The price of admission are some gold coins, the coins of love. Have you any?"

As this soul took out the coins, he had stored in his pockets, for this occasion, he saw that they had all turned into lead.

"How can this be? It makes no sense"

The angel smiled, "The coins I speak of, as said, are made of love. Your coins are made of earthly gold. There is a big difference."

Your gold, is a liability here and not an asset. We are miners for love, that is what we do here"

The angel then became a bright light and disappeared. The soul of the man wept, for at last he understood.

THE BURNING CANDLE

Now it was dark in the chamber, except for a single bright burning candle. One approached, who appeared forlorn and defeated. The angel enquired about his life and he explained how he had become a thief, during his time on earth and how he believed, he was not worthy to enter into heaven. However, the candle began to speak,

"Yes this man tells the truth, but I am burning because of the great love he had for his family. I burn because of the risks he took, in order to support them. How he spent many months in a cold jail, where icicles hung from the prison bars. Where he was beaten and humiliated. I burn because the economic conditions were so bad and the system so corrupt where he lived, this was all that was open for him to do. Otherwise his family would have starved."

Then the darkness spoke,

"You cannot let a thief enter the place of light, he belongs to us."

The angel answered, "he has already been in the darkness, yet his light shines, what good would he be to you?" The darkness recoiled and the candle burned even brighter. The angel led this soul through, to the great wonders of heaven.

THE PEARL

It is well understood, how in the natural world, a thing of great beauty can grow from its opposite. For example, the proverbial lotus, growing from the mud. Even small beautiful flowers can rise from a heap of dung. I have heard, one can see fields of flowers growing, where once terrible battles took place. Covering them in a carpet of yellow, or perhaps purple. Maybe in a way, this is true of our own lives as well. That is, at the end of them, despite all the challenges, we can show, we produced something of great beauty.

This is exactly what the humble oyster does. It lays on the sea bed, where a grain of sand or a parasite, finds it's way inside the oyster. This irritates it no end, but it has a very creative strategy, to deal with the intruder. It begins to coat it, with a substance called nacre or mother of pearl. It does this, one layer on top of another, for years, until a lovely pearl is formed. The bible calls this process, "beauty from ashes"

Another soul entered the heavenly chamber, to be greeted by an angel. He went on, to complain of his terrible life, one he said was filled with frustration and suffering.
The angel nodded in agreement, while consulting the GREAT TEXT OF SOULS. "But, what have you to show for it?" she turned to him.
The soul looked up, "nothing, I have nothing"
Then the angel did something, that could be perceived as, being quite extraordinary. She reached into the depths of his heart, emptying out all it's contents, salty water, which then fell to the floor of the chamber.
"This is the salt of all your many uncried tears," she added.
Upon seeing this and how he had lost the opportunity to do something positive with his former life, he wept, for what seemed to be an age. All the bitterness flowed out of him. He was made new again. Shiny, like a radiant pearl.

From the Great Text of the Souls:'The earthly heart is like a house with windows, and doors. Now when selfishness is an inhabitant, he will cover the windows and bolt all the doors, so the house will be dark, and no light can enter. Even when there is a tapping at the window, and a knocking at the door selfishness will refuse to answer.

However the Eternal will always knock on the door of every heart, for She longs to shine Her light into that heart and evict selfishness, and admit a new tenant therein, called love. For when love is a tenant in the house of the heart, fear will be afraid to enter and the swallows of joy will sing from it's rooftop and even the mortar between it's bricks will be called the bonds of trust.
Then when the winds of despair blow and the thunder of hate rages and the ground beneath the foundations roll like a wave - this house will stand strong. Now, when it becomes the time that the house of the heart has to die, if the tenant is love, she will remain, but if the tenant is selfishness, he will be buried in the rubble and the darkness.'

BEESWAX

Another entered. It was the soul of the cleaning lady. She had her head hunched over, from a lifetime of subservience, her skin toughened by hard work. This included her hands and knees, both which were rough and bore callouses. This was because, she often had to kneel for hours, day after day, performing her tasks. One beautiful thing the angel noticed, was that the scent of beeswax clung to her, like some invisible garment. It's perfume filled the chamber.

"Greetings," smiled the angel, who seemed happy to see her. The woman trembled a little, overwhelmed by the splendour of the celestial being, standing before her.

"There must be some mistake, I am not worthy to be here. This is a place fit for my mistress, not I"

Again the angel consulted THE GREAT TEXT OF SOULS and read how this woman had suffered terribly at the hands of a cruel employer. It spoke of how she had worked her fingers, almost to the bone for this rude and ungrateful mistress. Unbelievably, she did the work of two people, sometimes scrubbing the floors, by hand, of a whole palatial mansion. Instead of praise, she always received complaints, which she learned to bear with great dignity and without malice. The crowning jewel of her life, was her one child, a beautiful daughter, who she was determined to provide for. This, she reasoned, was the purpose for her life and compensation for her suffering.

Despite all this, she would often laugh out loud in a hearty voice. She took great pleasure in small luxuries, such as a glass of port, after a long day's work. She often prayed for others, especially her daughter.

And so, here she was, at the entry gates to heaven. The angel embraced her with his great wings, telling her that she would enter these gates, for this place was made for one such as her.

He added,

"Dear one, you were not so much cleaning and polishing the walls and floors of your mistress's house, but the very walls and floors of your own heart, which we can now all see, shines like the precious being you are"

When he was born, it soon became clear to his parents and friends, that he was a mute, a person who could not speak. This was accompanied by some hearing loss, but no one ever quite figured out, why Seth never uttered a word. It was endearing to some people, whilst others seemed unnerved by it. Seth kept it all in, he would watch everything, but never make a comment.

Now, upon finding himself in the unfamiliar surroundings of the heavenly chamber, facing an angel, feelings of awe rose up from within him. He couldn't help it, he opened his mouth to give praise and each word turned into an angel itself, which flew all about the chamber.

They flew in great joy, as if they had waited their whole lives to be released.

Our next soul, in his earthly incarnation, was a very small person. However, when he rose to the heavenly place, the angels, who are more aware of the soul than the body, thought he was a giant.

Many gathered to greet him, seeming to marvel at his size. This left him a little confused. "I am not a giant, you must be mistaken"

"Well, to us," an angel continued, "you are. It's what you have on the inside that counts."

"And you have a lot!" added another

Then there was great laughter in the chamber, as the angels led him through the gates and into heaven.

A pair of lovers died in a car accident, then rising to the heavenly chamber. They were surprised to see a silver thread connecting them, but it was explained to them that this signified their bond to one another.
An angel continued,

"It is difficult for the earthly mind to comprehend a tragedy such as yours. There will be many who will weep over your passing, but as you see it is just a passing from a place of life into the higher life. It is also difficult for you to comprehend that the time of your birth and passing is a part of a larger plan. Everything is moving from the lower to the higher, although it may not always appear to be so. You have known love and love comes from the highest, and may visit the lowest, and when she does, the joy is great."

The lovers were told that they were to be reborn, and would be lovers again in their new life on earth. They held hands and both drank from the river of forgetfulness.

BLANK FACES

Not everything that goes on in the heavenly chamber, is all light and love. Sometimes it falls on the angel to hold the mirror up to some dark souls. One such soul now waited in the wings. There is a lower chamber, but this soul was sent to the higher. There must've thought to be some redeeming qualities in him, to be sent to the higher chamber.

Let me also explain something. To a good and pure soul, the angel appeared the same. To a dark soul, the angel can appear frightening and foreboding. So when the soul was called to enter, he encountered a stern being, standing over a lectern, looking into a book called THE GREAT TEXT OF SOULS.

The angel looked up, "sit," she said. He felt he dare not disobey and sat on a stool on the other side of the room. She studied this book, for what seemed an eternity to him. It was a punishment in itself, yet he remained silent. After all, this was an unfamiliar place. He knew not of his future fate. Finally the angel looked up and then stared right into him, until he trembled with a great fear. There was nowhere to hide from that stare. The stare told him, she knew everything about his awful deeds on the earth. How he had evicted families into the winter cold, from properties he had owned. How he had bribed and cheated, without regard to any other person, so that he could get ahead. It was all in the great text, where the actions and thoughts of all souls are stored.

The angel led him to a scene, a kind've visual display, where they both witnessed those he had left on the earth. They watched as his family, friends and even his former mistresses, were fighting amongst themselves to try and get some more of the estate he'd left behind. The estate he worked so hard for, was now out of his control. It felt as though he'd sacrificed so much of his soul for so little. Land, title deeds, jewellery, share certificates. It all now seemed to him, to be so futile. "What are they doing?" he thought to himself. They all appeared to have blank faces.
He found it difficult to distinguish one person from another. It all looked so dark, there seemed to be no love on the earth for him. None at all. "What have I done?", he beseeched the angel in anguish. "Good, good," the angel answered, "your soul is re-emerging. It is never too late for repentance"
Suddenly, the small amount of light left inside his heart, exploded into a great joy, as he realised the great mercy given to him. He could've been left in the darkness, but was now in the light.

It could've been a boxing ring anywhere. Or, any one of a thousand boxers, who 'bought the bullet' that night. But, it was him, Jack, a 25 year old fighter, with prospects, in the prime of his life. This wasn't meant to happen. However, it was fate. His opponent had him on the ropes, after a lucky left to the head. It dazed him. He lost focus. Why didn't the ref stop the fight? stop the nearly 10 blows to the head? Who knows. It was too much to bear, as he fell to the ground, his heart stopped beating.

From this hellish scene, he rose into great peace and serenity. The fight, even his body laying there, drifted from his consciousness. He found himself in a heavenly realm surrounded by angels. Amazingly they knew all the details of his life and the fight that had just robbed him of his life.

Strangely, everything felt exactly as it should be. He reflected on all the events and people who had bought him to this point - the promoters, the crowd, his opponent, the odds, the heat of the lights. It all seemed like some kind of a symphony, where every note was in the right place.

"Hey," said one angel, "we're fighters too."
"But we fight for souls," said another
"Want to join us?" said the first, punching his fists in the air and smiling at the boxer.
"Yes, that's what I do," he added, "but when you punch like that, position your body like this"
The angels gave a knowing smile to one another. Then the boxer grew beautiful wings of his own, as there were many battles waiting.

In a far off place, that is hard for us to imagine, there stood, four soldiers. They had recently arrived at the portal to the heavenly realms.
They carried with them the acrid smell of gun powder. Black powder, has only a little smell, notes of charcoal mostly. The smoke from black powder is thick and white and it tastes like steam and sulphur. It filled the heavenly chamber. The rumble of distant cannon fire, shook the walls. It was punctuated by the unfortunate screams of the wounded and dying. These new arrivals came, from what many term, the theatre of war.

Three stood on one side of the chamber, while one remained on the other. The sounds of battle receded, It became clear, that the three were mortally wounded, by the soldier who stood alone.
It wasn't evident how the solo soldier lost his life, perhaps an unlucky stray bullet. What was clear, was that he was responsible for sending the others to the higher realms. Their wounds were grievous. One had lost his legs, one blinded and the other sustained a terrible stomach wound. However, it was now peaceful in the chamber. The lights of heaven, shining, as if, they were about to speak.

An angel appeared, enquiring of the three, "do you hold a grudge against the one who sent you here? You are the ones that have the power to pardon or condemn him"
Each one answered in turn, "No, we bear him no malice. If he didn't do this to us we would've done the same to him. He was doing his duty, as were we"
The four soldiers then embraced and wept together.

THE COMEDIAN

On the stage, he was one of the funniest guys you'd ever seen. Off stage, he could become sullen and morose. One side of his nature seemed to balance the other.
Because of these mood swings, he couldn't sustain a lasting relationship with anyone. He was aware, that he was impossible to live with. Maybe this was the reason he drank so much. There didn't seem to be a solution to his dilemma. It was a kind've joke to him. He didn't even try, but the money and fame grew. He was hailed as a comic genius, which in turn led to film parts. Not just small parts, but leading roles. Even hosting, the most prestigious film award nights. He used to look out at the audience and wonder why, they were laughing so much. He'd lost contact with the friends he started with. They were still struggling. It made him feel guilty. He thought many of them were more talented than himself. It didn't make any sense. So drinking

became an even bigger part of his life. There were times when he was so out of it, he'd forget everything. The world made sense then.

It was on a stormy night, that he contemplated ending it all. He thought it was funny, that it raged outside his window, adding a melodramatic touch.
He even laughed out loud. He hadn't laughed in a long time. He fully expected it to be the end, after he'd washed down a bottle of tablets, with a glass of red wine.
Floating above his bed, he wondered who that drunk guy was below him. Sleeping with all his clothes on, the TV still on. "Who is that deadbeat?" the question crossed his mind, He recognised it to be himself. "How can that be?"
Somehow his perspective grew beyond himself. He saw how he had bought joy to a lot of people. They loved him. 'Why didn't I know that?' he thought. He saw how he kept himself very small. He was good at keeping the love out. There was a celebration going on all around him, but he closed off to it. His heart was closed to everyone. Now, he could see clearly. It was as if he'd woken up.

An angel appeared before him. She smiled, saying, "Maybe the punchline is better than you thought it was"
"Maybe you're right" answered the comedian.

THE HOMECOMING

Her mind drifted through all the rooms she had spent most of her life in. They were never plush rooms, usually on highways or down market areas where the rent was cheap. she was married once, but couldn't adjust to suburban life and all that entailed. All she wanted to do was paint. She couldn't understand, so called, "normal people". "What do they fill their lives with?" she would ask of herself. "How can they not be filled with the desire to create?" She didn't care that her bed was hard, or the yellow cabs honked most of the time outside. She would often go hungry, to be able to afford her paints or the odd canvas. She had an account with a small fine arts shop, a suburb away. Often they would have bargains. She'd ride on the bus in her paint dappled overalls. Kids would laugh at her. She was oblivious to all that.

Sometimes she would even dance naked through her small flat, expressing the inner freedom she had in her heart. She was poor but happy. The smell of linseed oil and paints filled her flat. That unmistakeable smell. How could one ever explain? Sometimes she would sell a painting or two at an art show, yet she lamented that. She believed her works of art were her friends. One has to eat y'know

Now it happened in a flash. She wasn't looking, when she walked in front of the delivery truck. There was quite a commotion, yet she felt ecstatic. She was somewhere else. Suddenly she was standing in front of the place, she had always wanted to paint. There was a large oak tree in the middle of a vast field. The grass around it seemed alive, a colour she had never seen before. She felt more alive, than she had ever felt.

An angel flew over this field and hovered above her. Striking in it's majesty and the size of her wings. It was awesome to behold.

"this place was always within you, it was the place you were always reaching for, the place you were always trying to paint. Welcome home"

THORNS AND ROSES

The most precious and beautiful flower, the rose, with it's divine scent, is also surrounded by the sharpest thorns. Sometimes, when you are in the vicinity of such beauty, you can unfortunately experience the pain of being pierced by these thorns. Is the design of the rose an accident, or by divine will? That's for you to decide.

A young girl spoke to the attendant angel, in front of the heavenly gates. She explained, how she had been pierced by the thorns of love. She had loved another, but he didn't love her in return. She found the pain too difficult to bear and as a consequence, took her own life.
The angel took her by the hand, telling her, "we will walk on the pathway of love...come"
On the way they encountered a lone girl, who sat weeping, by a charred and burnt pine tree. The path then wound over

many cliffs, getting narrower all the time, until the angel cautioned, "Careful not to fall, watch your step, precious one" They passed, what seemed to be a thousand poets, all reading out aloud, beautiful love poems. The angel commented, "after one million years, they are no closer to describing love, than at the beginning" Large and shiny green serpents, writhed and snapped their teeth over their heads. "These are the beasts of jealousy," the angel told the girl. "Do not be afraid" On their way, they passed many bushes, made of thickets and thorns.

At last they came to the base of a hill, "follow me," beckoned the smiling angel. They both climbed this hill and getting to the top, were exposed to the most beautiful view. The whole valley was filled with the most exquisite rose bushes, as far as they both could see. The scent was so divine, all the wounds the girl had suffered, fell away and she was healed. Made anew, free to love again.

THE SINGER

Who can say why one person becomes rich and famous and another, perhaps a little less talented, is consigned to oblivion. It's in the "a little less" that there's a world of difference. That space can be filled with countless artists, musicians, entrepreneurs. It's in that small jump, that brilliance can be achieved. Who can define it?

We turn our minds, to the fate of one who achieved enormous success as a singer/composer. At the start, it didn't matter that he slept on a friend's floor, had a crumby guitar and busked on the grimy streets with 100 others. The talent he had within, shone out like a beam of light that illuminated other's hearts. First they would stand around him on the street, listening to his beautiful voice and melodies. Word got out. Soon he got some gigs in local coffeehouses, where the audience's were captivated by his songs and lyrics. Success seemed inevitable. It wasn't long before he was noticed by some TV execs, who put him on the small screen, which went out to millions of people worldwide.

From there, he went from strength to strength. But like the tip of an iceberg, the main part of this story was hidden from view. You see, for many many lifetimes, this soul had tried to breakthrough in the world, with his songs. Failure after failure, he learned a little more each time. The force and mass of his skill, built up until this current lifetime, where his gift burned with a fiery intensity. It happened to be at a time, when people needed it most.

A soul, sat by a river and gazed into it's waters. In these waters, she could see her future mother, father, sister and two brothers and this made her weep quietly. This soul would leave the scene and return many times, before deciding to be reborn. Eventually she drank from it's waters and disappeared. She knew of the various joys and travails she would have to face, but loved her earthly family more than heaven itself.

THE DARK PIT

A tyrant came,

"I was a conqueror of men and land and wasn't afraid of death. I am still unafraid. I don't believe in goodness - only greed is good. Greed turns the wheels of commerce and puts food on the table for peasant and king alike. The good are ripe for plunder, and like the fruit of a tree, I picked them at my leisure. I also sliced them in two when it suited my purpose. They cried to you, but you and yours abandoned them to me. I destroyed them, their wives and their children. I burned their homes to the ground and took their lands, yet you remained silent and distant like the stars."
His face changed, becoming a million faces, a leopard, a tiger and also many other beasts and men, the head of a prey mantis, a shark and various reptiles.
The angel responded,

"You have dispatched many souls here with your sword, it is true, but you only cut at their flesh and not their souls. The soul is like a river, you can strike it and cut it, yet it flows on unharmed. The soul is like the wind, you can try to cage it and tame it yet it laughs at your prisons and escapes. The soul is like the blue sky, you can try to lay title to it, or own it, but it is beyond title and cannot be owned or fenced in. These are powers beyond you."

The conquerer became enraged,
"Even these gates I will tear open with my sword," and he tried in vain, striking the gates with his sword, slashing and cutting as he leapt, but they closed up on him.

Another appeared in the angel's place. One that wore scales and carried the stench of foul flesh, one that breathed fire, and whose skin smouldered, and whose eyes were lifeless. A great and unfamiliar terror welled up in the conqueror's heart.
"You have earned me", it said, hissing out venom,
"I am your teacher and your understanding, and when you have learned to see beyond me, you will rise above me."
And they both disappeared down a deep dark pit.

THE WINNER

The winner? the loser? one seems dependant on the other. The gambling casinos are not set up to benefit the poor gambler. Obviously it's for the shareholders of the casinos, the online gambling portals, the poker machine owners. Each night, thousands, maybe more, of gamblers losses are converted into profits for these shareholders and owners. Sure, a gambler can win now and then, but this just encourages him, adds to the never ending fantasy, that he can eventually win big.

One such unfortunate, was a guy called Eddy. He'd been doing it so long, he hardly thought of anything or anybody else. He'd lost the family home, the wife, the kids, all who had lost respect for him, even hated him. Worse than a drunkard or drug addict, who could go through hundreds per day, Eddy could gamble away thousands, maybe more. Many times he got into trouble with the local mafia, but always managed to wriggle out somehow. He'd either have a win, or borrow money from some new friend he'd cultivated for that purpose. The gambling had seemed to drain all the goodness from his soul. His luck was about to run out. Borrowing from the wrong guy, who wasn't about to wait. Eddy couldn't find the money to pay this person, couldn't stitch the pieces together any more. In a strange way he was almost relieved, as this guy drew a gun on him. 'Do it,' he had the thought in his mind somewhere. Life had exhausted him, he hated himself so much, for how he had ended up. Bang! Surprisingly, it was all over so quick. Feeling an unexpected euphoria, the world disappeared from his mind. It became a play he had acted in. Did he do all that?

Many beings surrounded him in a circle. They were much larger than him and strangely, he seemed to recognise all of them. They all seemed to possess a bright inner light. One stepped forward and then Eddy's whole life appeared before him, like a kind've movie. It started from the time he was born. He saw himself as a child, a blessing to his parents. There was so much love there. He witnessed and felt the love his wife had for him when they were first married. As time moved on, he watched that precious love drain away, as he became more and more addicted to the gambling habit. He witnessed with great shame, his precious children, his friends and family lose their light for him. He was filled with a great agony. "Why did I do that? who on the earth loves me? No one? and for what?"

Suddenly, he found himself in a hospital bed. He heard the sound of traffic outside. "You were lucky to survive mate!" a voice said.

"Yeah, you were a million to one, odds on to not make it" said another

Eddy just smiled. He had a miraculous recovery. Better than they all expected. He never gambled again.

Again we head to the heavenly chamber, where the soul of a woman, we might call a glutton, made her entry. On her soul, as she had just arrived, she carried the impressions of the various foods she ate constantly. There was the smell of assorted meats, sweets, beers, soft drinks - a culinary smorgasbord. Mainly nutritionless foods.

The angel greeted her with an embrace, as the woman wept, "I couldn't stop eating. Believe me, I tried. It was something that was beyond me."

"You were trying to fill the emptiness you felt within. A seemingly bottomless pit"

"Yes," the woman answered, "you know it"

"Never mind we have a treat for you." He took her by the hand and led her to a banquet hall, where there was a table, covered with a white linen cloth. On it were various kinds of foods. They glistened and seemed to shine from within. The

angel then turned to her,
"This is the place where all hunger ends. None of these foods involved the suffering of any creature and you only have to eat them once, to be satisfied forever. They are for the nourishment of your soul"
The woman ate and was satisfied. Perhaps for the first time ever.

The angel told the landlord, "I see you were good to your tenants and would show compassion if they had difficulties. Now, as they were tenants in your house we are all tenants in the house of the Great Spirit."

She proceeded to lead him through to a large house that had a thatched roof and was by a small running stream. Tiny birds darted in and out of a garden and the sun light found it's way through the windows, painting the wooden floors with white light.
"Here there is no rent to pay and no lease to sign. You can stay here as long as you wish."

The landlord graciously accepted the angels offer and became a tenant in heaven

THE WALL

Often the same wall we build to protect ourselves, can also keep the good out. This is particularly true of the wall we build around our heart. We can be so keen on avoiding being hurt, we may scare off a genuine love or friend. How do we strike the right balance? Hmm

So, is the loss greater by the good we push away, or the not so good we may inadvertently let in? Another good question. In the case of our next entry into the forecourts of heaven, we meet someone, who all his life pushed it away. In fact, he had built quite a formidable wall around his heart.

An angel told him, if the flowers of the earth, did as you did, they could never grow. If they weren't exposed to the cold sleet, they would not feel the blessed rain, that helped them grow. If they did not feel the sun's rays on a hot day, they would not feel the perfect sunshine on a lovely day. Then the angel showed this soul, all the good he had pushed away in his life. The act of over protecting himself, had also hurt many others in the process.

"Do you want all of them to build walls too?" he was asked.
"The light comes in, when the walls come tumbling down. Yes you can get hurt trusting others, but you are more hurt, when you trust no one, for what have you become? A flower that does not grow, that receives not the blessed rain or sunshine"

"Dear angel, may I play you a tune,?" asked the musician. "Of course," she nodded and he proceeded to play her one of the most beautiful and uplifting melodies ever heard in the chamber. The angel danced in joy, saying, "Who has taught you to play like this?"
"My heart," the musician answered and the angel looked into the Great text of Souls and beheld the song of this soul's heart had filled many with joy and that the musician had no treasures on earth, but many behind the gates.

"Enter," sang the angel, dancing once again,
"The tune of your heart is understood on the earth and also in heaven."

A deformed woman stood before the angel, saying, "I am so ashamed. My appearance during my earthly life was so unattractive. When I was a child other children made fun of me and when I became a woman there was no one who wanted my company. Because of this I was alone and distressed."
The angel held up a mirror in front of this poor soul, who when she looked into it, saw one of exceeeding beauty.

"Who is this?," she asked in awe of the reflection.
"This is your soul," answered the smiling angel.

The woman wept for what seemed like an eternity and then she entered the gates with the angel.

RELIGIOUS ITEMS

A man climbed a ladder all the way to heaven. He carried many religious items, including a prayer shawl, some incense holders, prayer books, a prayer mat, a number of statuettes and various pictures of holy people.

An angel greeted him, when he arrived, "It must be difficult to climb the ladder to heaven and carry all these things - why don't you let them go and come on in?"

The man stared, as if in shock, "Let go of my beloved traditions. I can't." he bowed his head and fell back down, to the earth.

Another man climbed a ladder all the way to heaven. This ladder was constructed from the many prayers he had performed during his lifetime. Explaining to the angels he met there, "I prayed through everything that happened to me, the good, the bad, the fortunate and the disastrous.
Many winds and storms threatened to throw me to the ground, but I kept climbing"
"Well here you are then," answered the beautiful winged being. The man kicked the ladder away and climbed into heaven.

He was a very good juggler. He worked at fairs and on the streets, wherever he could make a buck. He could juggle 5 things at a time, to the astonishment of the crowds watching. Even standing on one leg, was no challenge for him. Sometimes, he could even stand on his head and juggle 3 things with his feet.

One night in a dream, he saw how all the planets, the suns, asteroids, cells in the body, everything, everything, were all held in place by a master juggler. It was astonishing to him. It filled him with awe, this realisation. How was this possible? I have never thought of things in this way. Who or what is responsible for keeping everything in it's place?

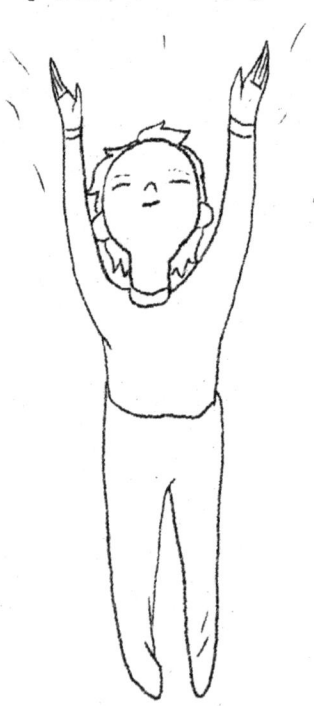

THE FATHER OF ALL THINGS

A small child entered the chamber and she said, "I was cut down before I had a chance to live."

"Then you shall live forever behind these gates, or return to live the many years of life you were denied below.
Which is it to be?"
"I want my father," the soul of the child cried.
The gates opened wide and many children led this soul by the hand to the Great Spirit, who is the Father of all things."

A beautiful woman who passed over, was quite shocked to find that she didn't have a body, "Where is my beautiful face?" she screamed, "my long legs and polished fingernails? Oh my God, am I in hell?"

An angel appeared and answered her, "What you are, is here with you now. You are not your body, you are your soul and this is the place where all souls must come, when they either enter the higher realms of light or return back to the worlds of matter."

"I don't care about that, I want to be the way I was."

She drank from the river of forgetfulness and returned to be reborn once again.

THE ADDICT

Heroine, smack, snow, dope, horse. Doesn't matter what you called it, for him it was sublime. Took him to the gates of heaven, then bought him down with a crash.
His life had become a never ending search for the stuff. It didn't start out like that. In fact, he was a respectable doctor, with unfettered access to morphine.
Because morphine can come in white tablets to be taken orally, the tablets are often called the white lady. They are also called salt and sugar. That's where it all started. He soon got used to these and wanted something stronger. This is what drove him to the streets at night, to liase with dealers to get hold of some smack. Needless to say, he lost his po-

sition as a doctor. There was a big scandal. It was in all the papers DR SO AND SO, DRUG ADDICT.

So down and down he went, into the descending spiral. Somewhere inside himself, he knew what he'd become. Someone, who would sell his mother for another hit of the drug. In all these stories, it can be seen, there are many ways up and many ways down. He found himself, laying on a bed somewhere, looking out a window. A busted spring from the mattress stuck into his back. He didn't care. It was the least of his problems. Across from him, there were children laughing and playing in a park. The sun was shining. He felt he was looking at another world, not his world. There was a constant hunger and gnawing in his stomach, as if a demon lived inside him.

He fell asleep, he was so tired. Finding himself, standing at the foot of some huge gates, which he intuitively recognised as the gates of heaven. He watched as many angels came and went. They didn't seem to see him. "Perhaps I have no soul," he reasoned. One angel flew towards him. "That is partly true. There are no shortcuts to heaven. You cannot enter. Your vibration has been altered to be much lower than it should be. You think there is heaven in the substances you took? The opposite is true. You have the choice to return, give up these things, or be reborn to face the same circumstances again, but choose the right path. The path back to us"

He felt such peace and asked if he returned, was there was a way he could remember the angel's face. She responded, that her face was in the face of a flower, the rays of the sun and the laughter of the children. You will remember," she answered

Soon he was back in the bed with the broken mattress, the spring sticking into his back. The inner gnawing had gone. The world looked different.

WEALTH AND KINDNESS

A man appeared before the angel, one who had enjoyed great wealth in his life, yet had also been kind and compassionate.

The angel beckoned, "Do you wish to join us here, or return to the world below? It is your choice."

This man decided the good he knew, was worth more than the good he had no knowledge of. So he agreed to drink from the river of forgetfulness, whereupon he disappeared.

Yet another knocked on the door.

The angel recognised him, for she knew of this holy soul. As she looked into the Great Text of Souls she saw that it bore witness to this man's great strength and kindness. "You are held in high esteem here," she smiled reassuringly, "and many have been illuminated by your great light, but there is a less developed soul by your side, yet one who has enough merit to enter. However, we only have room for one. You tell me…" enquired the angel, "who should enter? you or the one beside you?"

The holyman trembled and bowed his head,
"Oh angel of the Eternal, let him who is by my side enter."
With that a great light appeared, brighter than the angel or the holyman had ever seen.
It seemed infinite in it's radiance, yet at the same time, small and intimate. It spoke in tones that roared like the ocean, yet sounded like a soft whisper,

"By My name
both shall enter,
for by Myself
were all things created
and by Me are all redeemed."

The hearts of the two men and the angel pulsated with love and were joyful beyond measure.

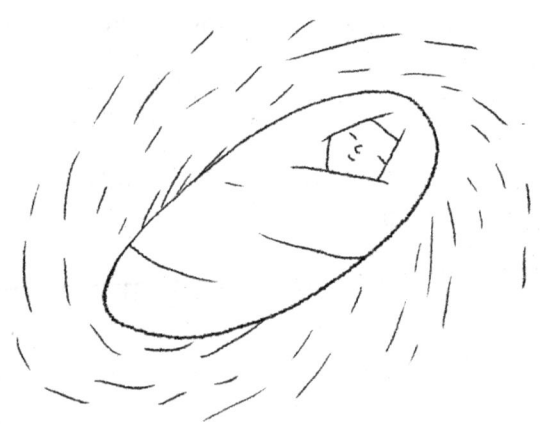

SOMETHING SPECIAL

And it came to pass that the angel was summoned before the Eternal,

"My beloved, many souls have you processed and you are one of the ones with great merit, one of the vessels I dwell in, yet the earth slips further from Me by their own choice, which I have given to them as a gift.

You will return as flesh to that place where distance is not measured by spirit but by mass, which they have chosen to see. You will be a stranger to some and a light to many and also cursed by many, but this is the way of strength - the way of the lamb."

And in a little town upon the face of the earth, the cry of an infant broke the stillness of night. Many animals became still also and even the fish in the sea knew something special was happening

The Olive Grove

If you were standing there, at that time, you might've heard his footsteps climbing the pathway up to the olive grove. A light click clack, of his sandals, soft but firm. It came from far away, then grew louder. His face became more visible, it had a Mediterranean appearance.

The sides of the pathway were stone. On the upper side of the path was the olive grove and on the lower side was a paddock, sparsely populated with sheep. Darkness was falling, the shadows were deepening.

Now the pathway was lit by moonlight and his footsteps grew louder, some of them kicked up a little dust. The scene was still, apart from the random bleating of a single sheep now and then.

His face came closer into view, it was at once kind and soft and also had the appearance of being made from sculpted stone, a walking paradox when you looked at him. It played with your mind.

There was a kind of strength and power mixed with extreme tenderness. He appeared alone but there was a fullness to him, as if an invisible legion walked by his side. He climbed up the path to the grove, then stood by an olive tree and touched several leaves, twisting them gently in his fingers.

Now the darkness replaced the dusk and he laid down in the grove. A slight breeze blew among the trees and then ceased. He fell asleep.

In the darkness wild hyenas came near, but his presence calmed them and they did nothing to harm him. The same was true of the vipers who lived in and about the grove.

All became very still, as he rested on the face of the earth.

THE BEGINNING

Another book by Pietr
Inside every heart shines a beautiful star
with words by Pietr and beautiful sketches by
Marie Muravski. If you're interested in ordering
this, please write to:
shakeatambourine@gmail.com

www.ingramcontent.com/pod-product-compliance
Lightning Source LLC
Chambersburg PA
CBHW060216050426
42446CB00013B/3087